C000053096

ORO Editions
Publishers of Architecture, Art, and Design
Gordon Goff: Publisher

USA, ASIA, EUROPE, MIDDLE EAST
www.oroeditions.com
info@oroeditions.com

Copyright © 2013 by ORO Editions
ISBN: 978-1-935935-82-7

Production Manager: Usana Shadday
Color Separations and Printing: ORO Group Ltd.
Printed in China.

Text printed using offset sheetfed printing process in 4 color on
157gsm premium matt art paper with an off-line gloss acqueous
spot varnish applied to all photographs.

ORO Editions has made every effort to minimize the overall
carbon footprint of this project. As part of this goal, ORO Editions,
in association with Global ReLeaf, have arranged to plant two trees
for each and every tree used in the manufacturing of the paper
produced for this book. Global ReLeaf is an international campaign
run by American Forests, the nation's oldest nonprofit conservation
organization. Global ReLeaf is American Forests' education and
action program that helps individuals, organizations, agencies, and
corporations improve the local and global environment by planting
and caring for trees.

North American Distribution:
Actar Distribution
151 Grand Street, 5th Fl.
New York NY 10013, USA
www.actar-d.com

International Distribution: www.oroeditions.com/distribution

Books in this series

0424 WESTCHESTER COMMUNITY COLLEGE
GATEWAY CENTER

This is one in a series of books, each of which tells
the story of a single building. It is our hope that
as these books accumulate alongside our body of
work, they, in their aggregate, will form a profile of
our design intentions.

Ennead Architects

GATEWAY

Visiting Westchester Community College for the first time on a hot summer day in 2004, I was taken by the beauty and stillness of the verdant campus and the remnants of its historical roots as an early twentieth-century country estate.

The campus is situated in the hamlet of Valhalla, twenty-five miles northeast of New York City. Legend has it that the name of the town was inspired by Richard Wagner's "Ring" cycle opera. In Norse mythology, the place was reserved in the afterlife for noble warriors. The present day Valhalla is coincidentally famous in the region for being the final resting place for numerous well-known people in the four neighboring cemeteries.

That Westchester County had purchased the estate in 1957 and that it has become a thriving community college is a wonderful transformation: this beautiful landscape has been opened to the public for the sole purpose of educating local residents. Since its founding, the College has become an important institution in the community, currently educating upwards of 10,000 students yearly. More recently, it has become the primary point of access to an American college education for thousands of immigrants to the county. Becoming involved as the architects for the new Gateway Center was a tremendous opportunity for us to support and reinforce the College's vision to further enhance access to the campus for these students and to provide new classes and programs that would better serve the diverse and growing community of non-English speakers. We sought to create a building that would symbolize that vision and fulfill the College's aspirations to create a new threshold and center on campus.

The design for the building was inspired by the site's subtle rolling topography, its history and the importance of providing local access to higher education for residents of Westchester County. To achieve this, the design concept weaves together spaces for learning and community gathering with the enveloping landscape, historical references to the original estate, daylight, local materials and color. The design fuses the building with the site — framing and securing the environment, while defining a vital crossroads on campus. Experiencing and engaging the building is intended to heighten an awareness of the value and beauty of the surrounding landscape. This experience is further intensified by unifying interior and exterior — drawing students and visitors into a dialogue with the change of the seasons and the passage of the day. As a symbol of openness and accessibility, the transparent Gateway volume is intended to mark the intersection of the College and the community — to define the physical embodiment of GATEWAY and, through it, access to education and opportunity.

Susan T. Rodriguez
March 2013

HISTORY

Westchester Community College was founded in 1946 as the New York State Institute of Applied Arts and Sciences in White Plains. In 1957, the County of Westchester bought a 360-acre estate in Valhalla and designated 218 acres for the College.

Hartford Hall, the original residence on the estate, was completed in 1932 and designated a National Historic Preservation Site in 1978. Formerly called Buena Vista Farms, the Tudor-style home was the residence of John Hartford, the longtime President of the A&P grocery store chain. The building is currently home to the President's office and College administration and defines the central campus core.

Westchester Community College campus

A community college is all about: classes for vocation and avocation, providing the means for individuals to improve themselves. Here they take affordable classes to make something of themselves. Some go on directly to careers, others move on to four-year institutions. Still others just take a class or two to get more meaning out of life.
- Joseph N. Hankin

MOVING YOUR INSTITUTION INTO THE 21ST CENTURY

Community college student populations are becoming more diverse, which of course has implications for all aspects of an institution. No longer are we catering only to recent high school graduates during the day hours, and part-time students at night, but typical community colleges serve a myriad of societal groups throughout the day and week, including weekends, and at off-campus locations: housewives, employees requiring upgrading of skills, special high school populations including those "at-risk," (or those who have already dropped out), small business owners, dislocated workers including some who are not literate, immigrants requiring English-as-a-second-language courses, international students, non-credit students, disabled students, shut-ins, GED seekers, students who come to us with either advanced degrees or some college (reverse transfer students) or proficiency in skills such as computer skills, senior citizens, children who want to participate in special interest programs, avocational learners who are not seeking professional advancement but are willing to pay for courses related to their leisure interests, and many others. A true community college has a student profile that matches closely the contours of the community population in its service area.

We could take a leaf from the book of marketers of commercial products. For example, car companies are selling a person her or his own sense of self-esteem, power, freedom, emotion, security and status. If you think about those characteristics, the same thing is true of colleges trying to sell courses. People take them for different reasons, and it is up to us to isolate those reasons.

Business and industry have segmented their markets, and we also should do so as we look for new populations. There are family households, singles, female-headed households with children under 18, blacks and Hispanics, downscale and upscale households, dual-earning couples, honeymooners, just couples, new parents, full-nesters, young families, empty nesters, old money, conspicuous consumers, baby boomers, condominium dwellers, third world melting pots or mosaics, family sports and leisure lovers, golden year retirees, small town families, mobile home dwellers, farm families, military base families, and many other categories — all potential markets for an enterprising college.

John Gardner has told us that "Sometimes our institutions are like sand dunes in the desert — shaped more by influences than by purposes." The message for those of us who plan to be around to anticipate the changes in the future is clear: we can create our own future, but we have to see clearly what changes are occurring, and think clearly what our purposes are so we remain loyal to our philosophy as institutions of lifelong learning. Surely our colleges are fulfilling the promise of the Statue of Liberty, as George Vaughan has indicated:

Give us your young, and your not so young;
Give us your capable, and your not so capable;
Give us your minorities, and your homemakers;
Give us your employed, your underemployed, your unemployed;
Give us those in society who have too long lingered on the periphery of the American dream,
And we will help them to become better students, better workers, better citizens, better people.

Joseph N. Hankin
President of Westchester Community College since 1971

CHANGING DEMOGRAPHICS: Westchester County and New York City

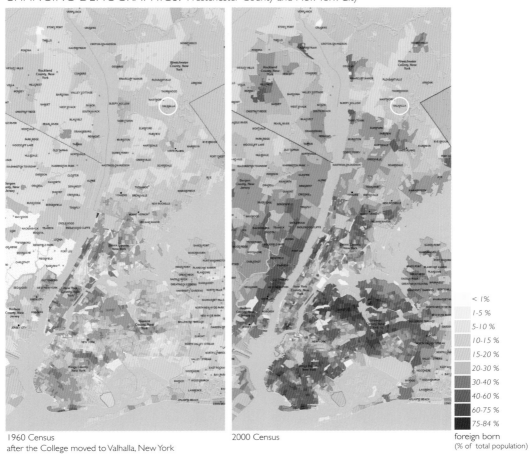

1960 Census
after the College moved to Valhalla, New York

2000 Census

foreign born
(% of total population)

< 1%
1-5 %
5-10 %
10-15 %
15-20 %
20-30 %
30-40 %
40-60 %
60-75 %
75-84 %

*Accessibility is my most important achievement. When I first came to
the College, there was a barbed wire fence around it. After I accept-
ed the position, one of the first things I did was tear that fence down
so we would be more accessible to the public.*
- Joseph N. Hankin

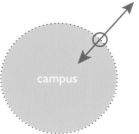

A COMMUTER CAMPUS

Located in the suburbs north of New York City, Westchester Community College provides post-secondary
education to a diverse and ever-changing population.
The commuter school's main campus is located in
Valhalla, with extension centers throughout the County.
Access to the campus is dependent on vehicular transportation and a network of county roadways.

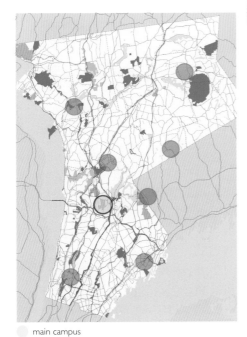

⬤ main campus
⬤ extension center

13

The realities of a commuter campus in a suburban environment demand that vast areas of the campus be dedicated to parking. Over the years, the school's park-like character has been impacted dramatically to accommodate parking lots.

parking lots ■

green space

GREEN SPACE

PRESERVING AND FRAMING THE LANDSCAPE

| 1 story | 2 stories | 3 stories |

scale of building on site

Preserving and celebrating the existing landscape were important considerations in the design and siting of the building. A principal goal was for the building to engage the land with minimal disruption to the natural context and historical setting.

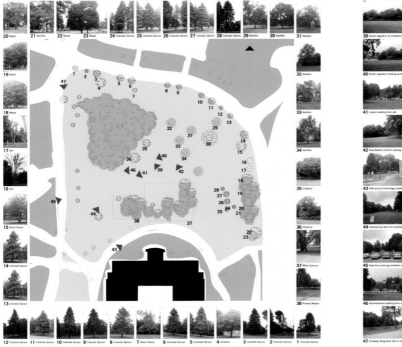

inventory of site vegetation

17

PROGRAM

The program for the building was developed in response to greater student diversity and a growing demand for professional training from area businesses. The program includes spaces that support the international student community's transition to American culture and spaces that accommodate business instruction for the local workforce. The College's academic departments dedicated to language and business support the vision for the building. Included are: the "Language Cluster," which houses the Modern Languages Department, the English Language Institute and Mentoring and Conversational Partners; and the "Business Cluster," which includes the Business Department, Professional Development Center and the fashion program. A third "Welcome Cluster" includes the Welcome Center and the International Student Office and serves as the main public interface for visitors to the building and the campus overall. In addition, general classrooms and seminar rooms are available to accommodate the increasing enrollment at the College. The remaining components of the program include shared gathering spaces intended to foster communication and build community.

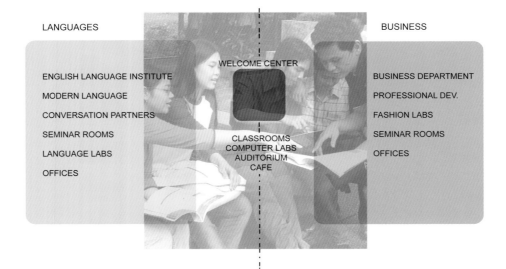

LANGUAGES

WELCOME CENTER

BUSINESS

ENGLISH LANGUAGE INSTITUTE

MODERN LANGUAGE

CONVERSATION PARTNERS

SEMINAR ROOMS

LANGUAGE LABS

OFFICES

CLASSROOMS
COMPUTER LABS
AUDITORIUM
CAFE

BUSINESS DEPARTMENT

PROFESSIONAL DEV.

FASHION LABS

SEMINAR ROOMS

OFFICES

ASSEMBLY PROGRAMS   4,900 SF

ASSEMBLY
4,900 SF

WELCOME CLUSTER   2,470 SF

INTERNATIONAL
STUDENT
OFFICE
640 SF

WELCOME
CENTER
1,830 SF

LANGUAGE CLUSTER   8,145 SF

LOUNGE /
CONVERSATION
AREAS

ENGLISH
LANGUAGE
INSTITUTE
4,445 SF

MODERN
LANGUAGES
2,820 SF

MENTOR AND
CONVERSATION
PARTNERS
880 SF

PROFESSIONAL CLUSTER   9,310 SF

LOUNGE /
CONVERSATION
AREAS
(PART OF CIRCULATION)

BUSINESS
DEPARTMENT
4,440 SF

PROFESSIONAL
DEVELOPMENT
OFFICE
4,870 SF

GENERAL PROGRAMS   17,000 SF

UNASSIGNED
FACULTY OFFICES
1,100 SF

SHARED
CLASSROOMS
15,000 SF

SUPPORT
SPACES
900 SF

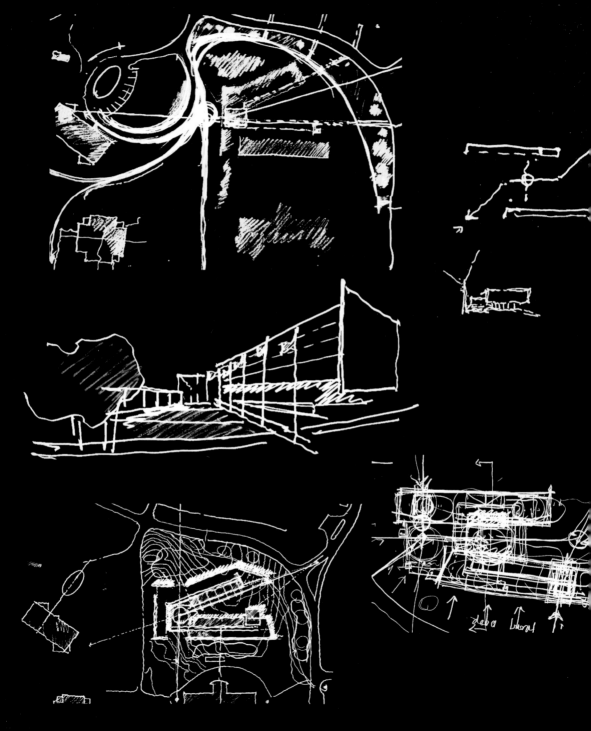

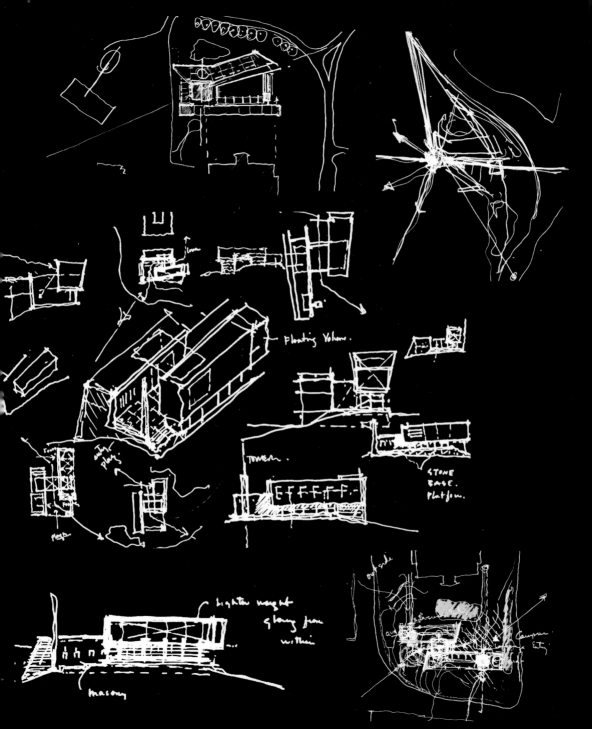

DEFINING GATEWAY

In response to the demand for greater access to
education, the College envisioned a new threshold
building that would reinforce the relationship
between community and campus. The Gateway
Center was created as a unique educational crossroads and a defining center for campus life. Sited
to take advantage of the natural beauty of the
campus landscape, the Gateway Center serves as
the threshold to the College and an initial expres-
sion of campus identity.

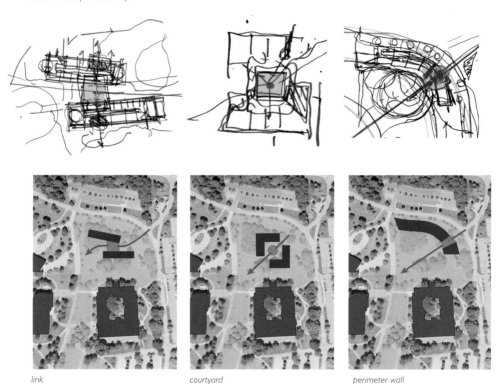

link　　　　　　　　　　　*courtyard*　　　　　　　　　　　*perimeter wall*

22

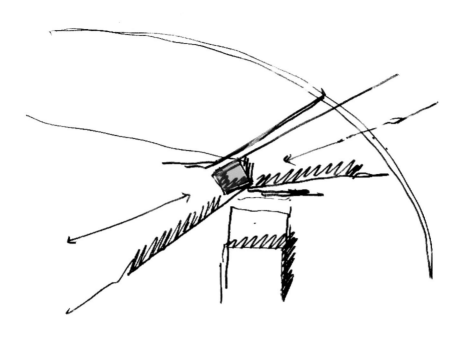

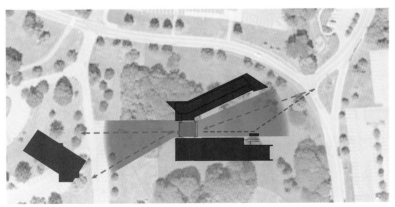

link and focus

ENGAGING TYPOGRAPHY

The concept evolved to resolve the sloping
topography of the site by marking the sectional
overlap of the two levels with a 48-foot-tall floating
glass volume that forms the primary entry to the
building and connects the north and south wings
at two levels. This pavilion provides a physical place
for gathering and is the intersection of community
and campus life. To the east, a tower reinforces the
building's identity as the gateway to the College.

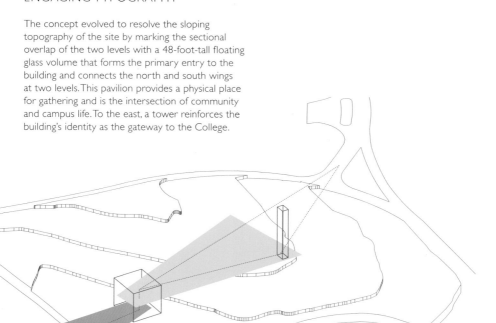

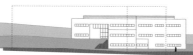

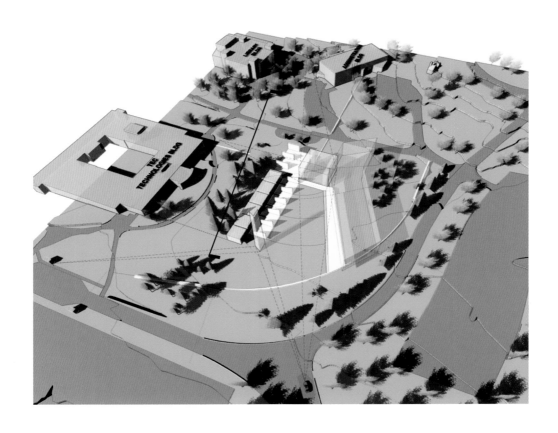

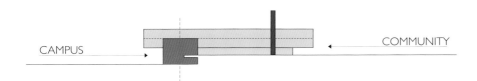

CAMPUS

COMMUNITY

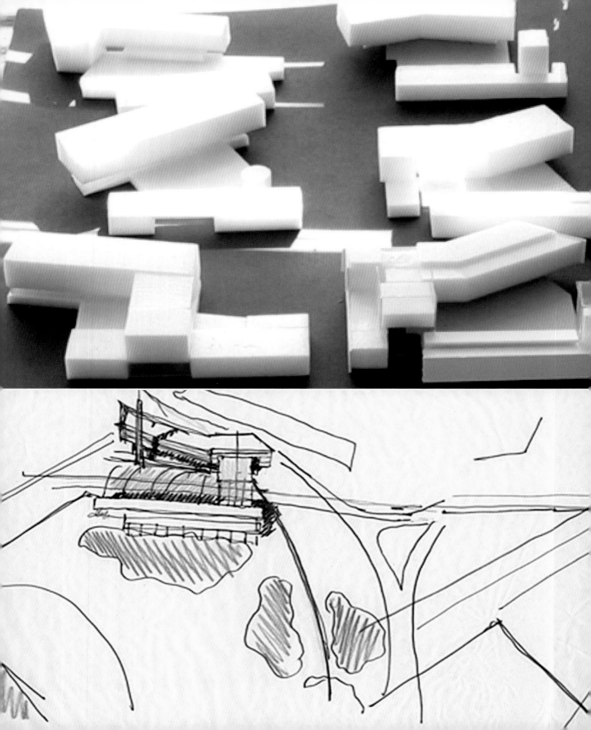

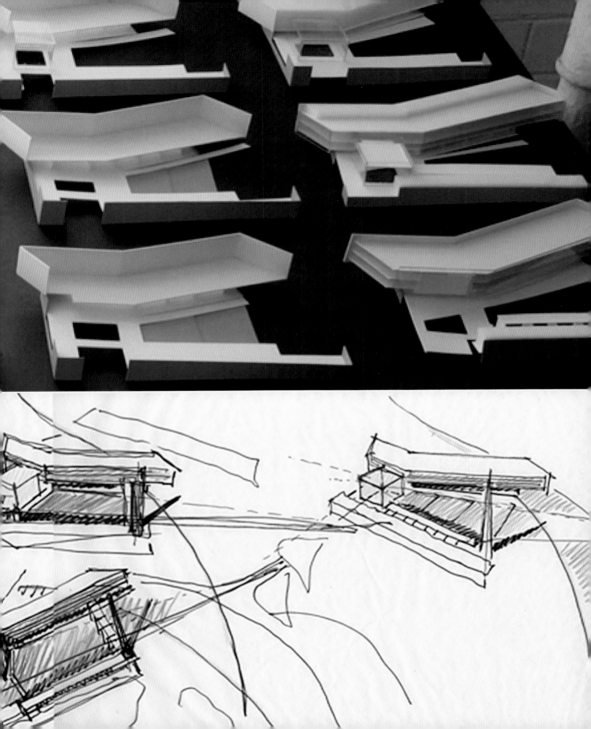

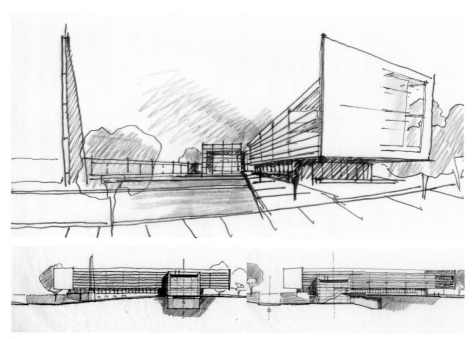

The two-story structure to the south houses the language program, general classrooms and faculty offices. The three-story structure to the north houses the auditorium, general classrooms and faculty offices for the business and fashion programs. The Gateway unifies the two wings of the building and mediates a grade change across the site from east to west.

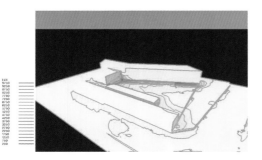

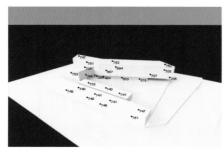

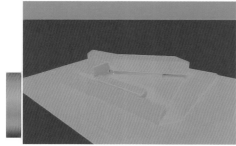

solar studies

SUSTAINABLE DESIGN

Sustainable design principles informed the design from the overall siting and massing strategy to the integration of energy-efficient systems, the detail development and selection of materials. The building has achieved LEED Gold Certification. Sustainable highlights include: minimizing site disruption by integrating the building into the natural topography and preserving existing trees; maintaining a vegetated open space around the building to reduce stormwater run-off and heat island effect; and providing a natural habitat for flora and fauna and a stormwater system to capture and treat runoff in four bioretention basins before discharging it to the campus-wide stormwater system. Additionally, water efficiency is achieved through the use of native and adaptive plant species, eliminating the need for irrigation. The building's solar orientation and fenestration enhance daylight within the building. Operable windows throughout contribute to enhanced indoor air quality. A high-performance exterior envelope mitigates heat gain and reduces energy consumption with custom-designed sunscreens on the south façade and Low E glazing throughout. Locally quarried stone is a featured material of the building. High-performance mechanical systems, lighting controls and glazing will save over 30% of fossil fuel and electricity consumption annually. Waste management during construction achieved a 90% recycling rate. A carbon dioxide monitoring system provides feedback on the ventilation system. Access to public transportation is adjacent to the site.

COMPONENTS

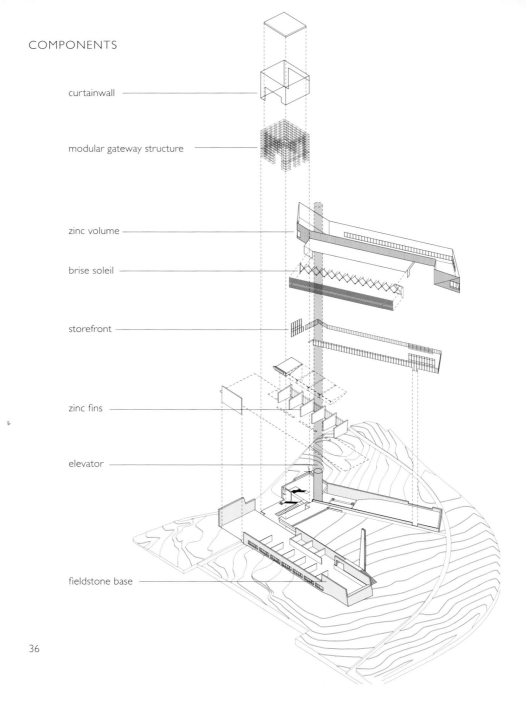

curtainwall

modular gateway structure

zinc volume

brise soleil

storefront

zinc fins

elevator

fieldstone base

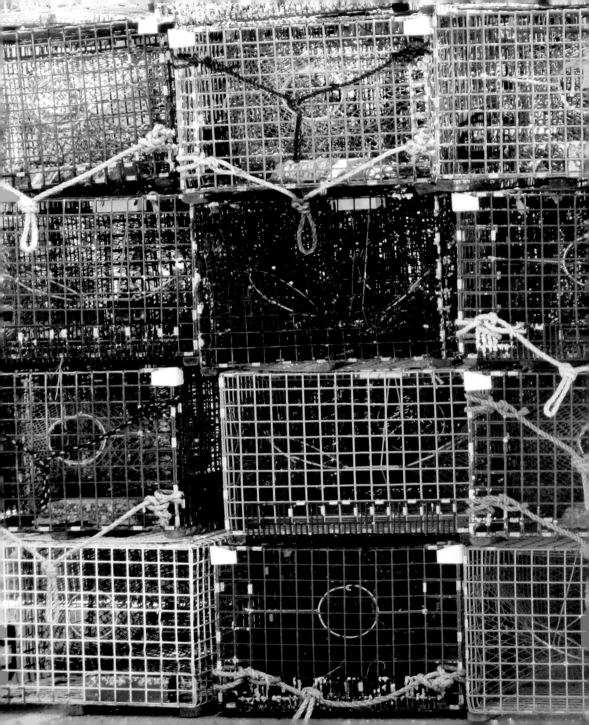

MODULAR GATEWAY STRUCTURE

A modular, prefabricated system defines the structural framework of the glass pavilion. Two hundred thirty-three architecturally exposed structural steel "boxes" were assembled to create a light, transparent volume. Based on eight basic templates, which maximize repetition and efficiency in the shop, the boxes were fabricated from channels and plates. Field connections were made with shims and bolts, cutting down erection time by minimizing the amount of field welding. Curtain wall connections were made to steel plate tabs that were attached to the boxes in the shop.

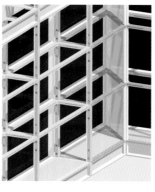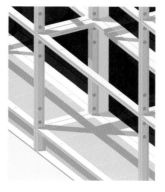

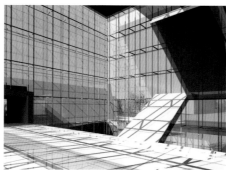

The pavilion's primary staircase and the bridge linking the north and south wings of the building are made with laminated glass panels. The bridge is supported in part by two steel hanger rods that connect to the main stringers with custom pin and jaw fittings.

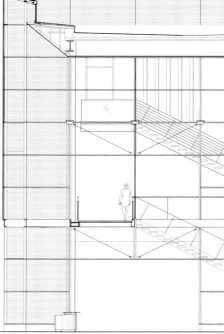

stair detail

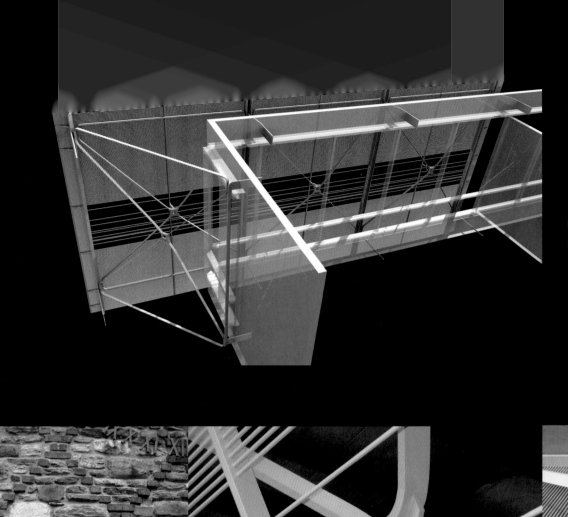

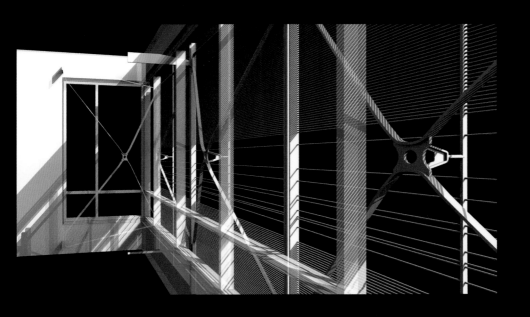

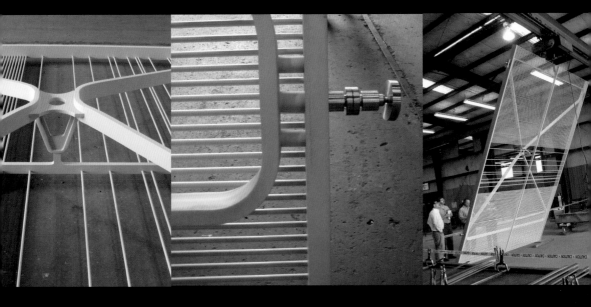

BRISE SOLEIL

The diagonal bracing in the brise soleil on the Gateway Center's south-facing courtyard façade references the brick patterning of historic Hartford Hall. The screen allows building inhabitants undisrupted views of the campus while optimizing natural daylight and reducing glare.

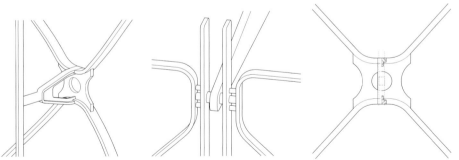

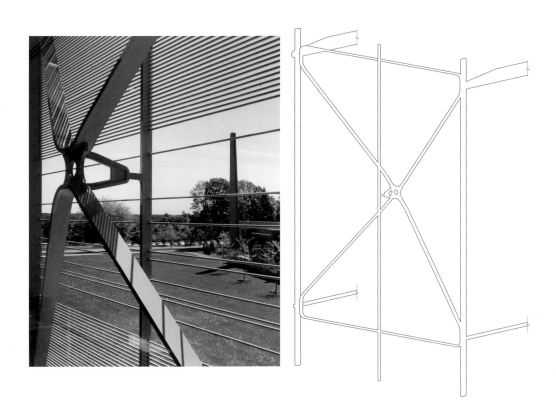

CANTILEVER

At the eastern end of the building, the third floor cantilevers over its base on all sides, with lengths varying from six to thirty feet.

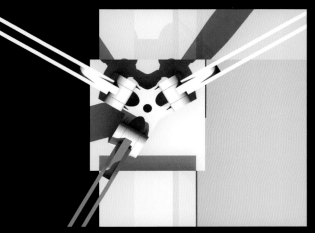

On the western end, the cantilever is relieved by an inverted tripod; three legs are supported on a steel column embedded in a concrete wall below. Each leg consists of two parallel plates stitched together at regular intervals with round spacer bars, creating ladder-like elements. To eliminate bending forces in the tripod, each leg terminates in a steel pin detail. The pins, four inches in diameter, are tied together at the base by a plate assembly designed to transmit gravity and lateral forces to the concrete structure below.

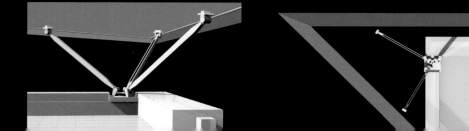

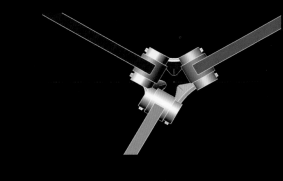

MOVEMENT

Circulation spaces throughout the building provide
places for gathering and views to the landscape.
Regular seating nooks and syncopated wall place-
ment animate the hallways.

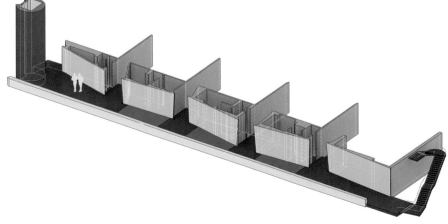

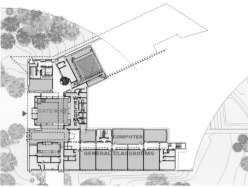

campus level plan

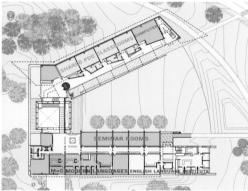

terrace level plan

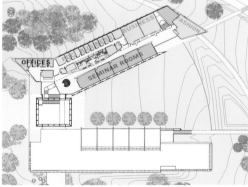

third level plan

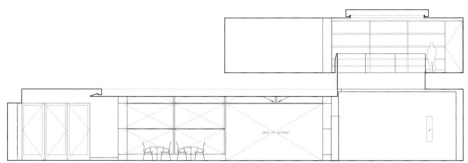

double-height section through café

DRAWINGS

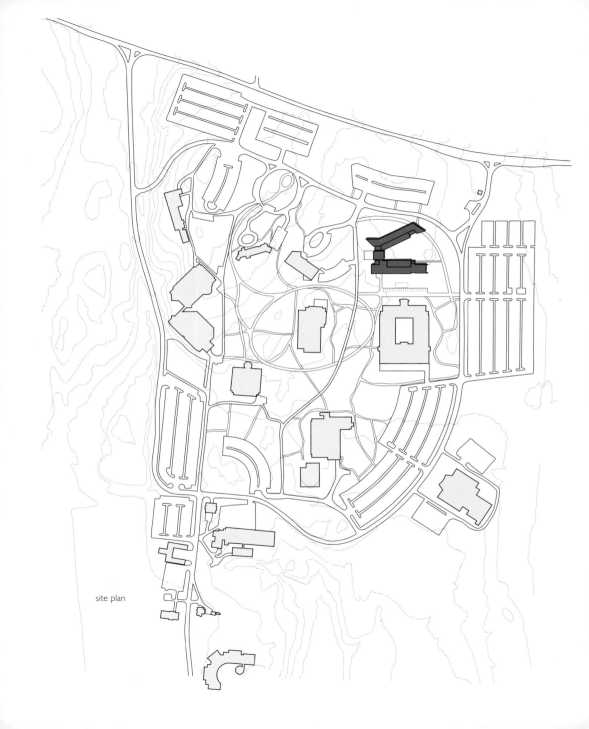

site plan

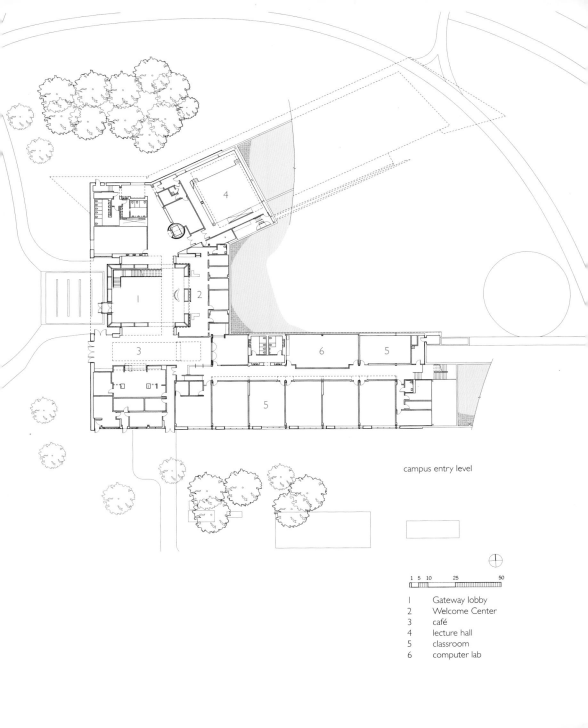

campus entry level

1   Gateway lobby
2   Welcome Center
3   café
4   lecture hall
5   classroom
6   computer lab

1 5 10   25   50

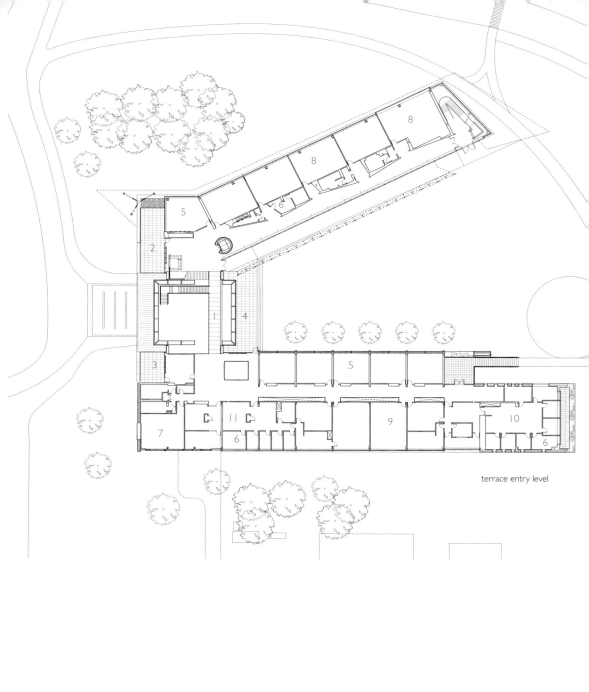

terrace entry level

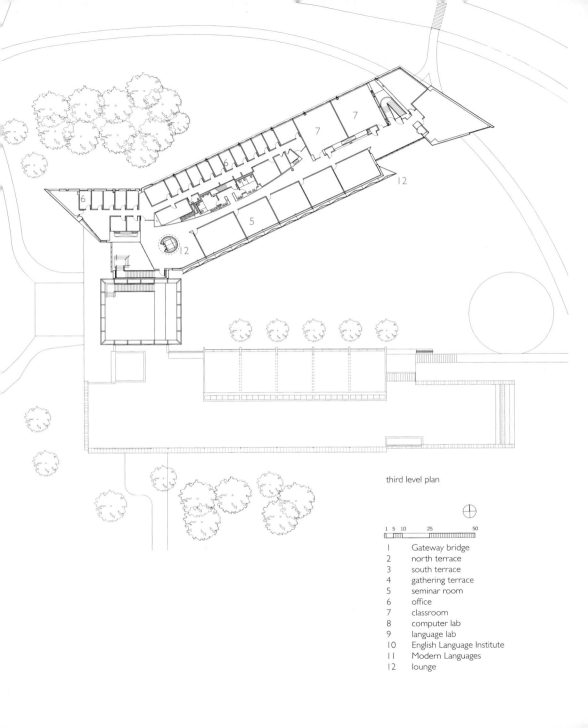

third level plan

1 5 10   25   50

1   Gateway bridge
2   north terrace
3   south terrace
4   gathering terrace
5   seminar room
6   office
7   classroom
8   computer lab
9   language lab
10 English Language Institute
11 Modern Languages
12 lounge

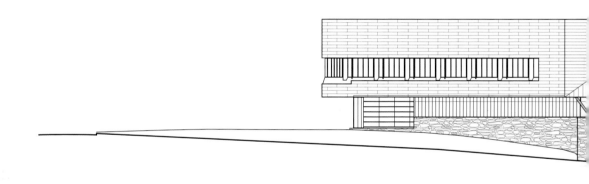

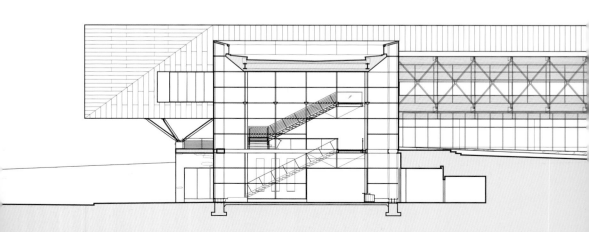

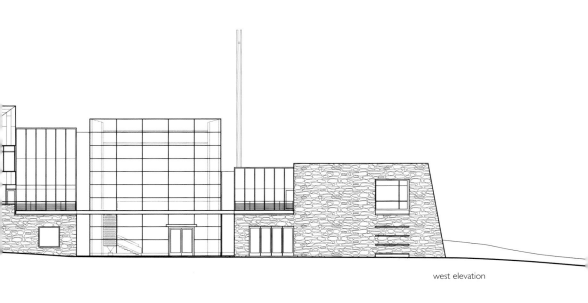

west elevation

building section/south elevation, north wing

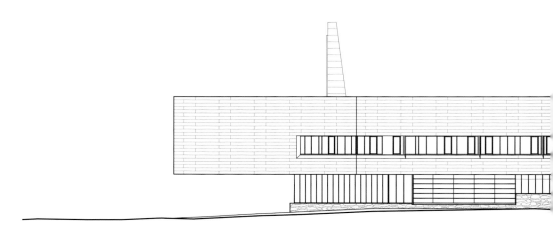

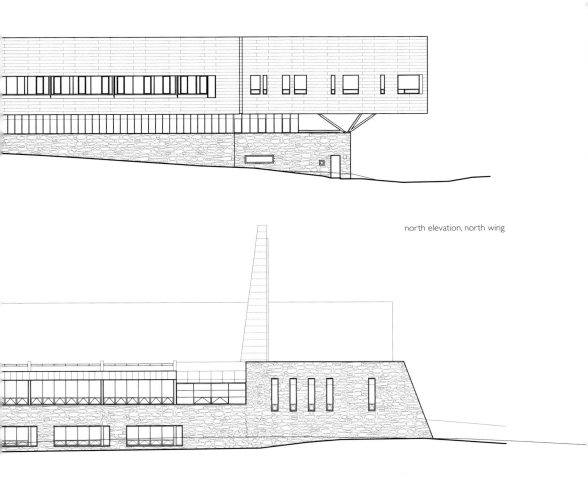

north elevation, north wing

south elevation, south wing

east elevation

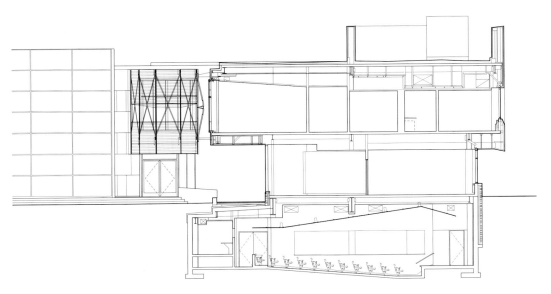

section through north wing looking west

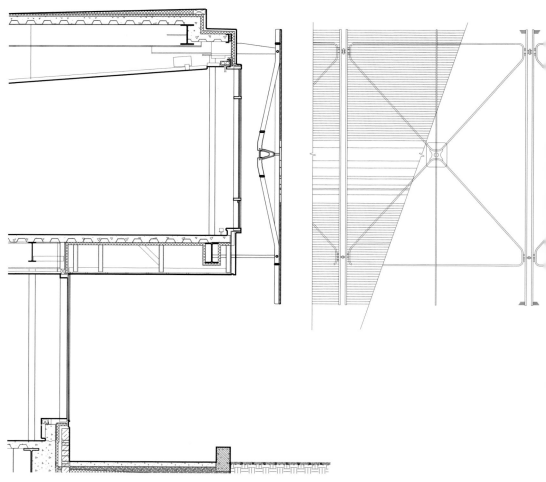

wall section

CLIENT
Westchester Community College

ENNEAD ARCHITECTS
Design Team: Susan T. Rodriguez, Timothy Hartung, Joanne Sliker, John Zimmer, Patrick Golden, Harry Park, Craig McIlhenny, Mimi Madigan, Paul Keene, Charles Brainerd, Maura Rogers, Kyo-Young Jin, Yekta Pakdaman-Hamedani, Matthew Bissen, Saem Oh, Charmian Place, Joerg Kiesow, Daniel Stube

CONSULTANTS

Structural	LERA
MEP	Thomas Polise Consulting Engineer
Landscape	Towers | Golde
Lighting	Susan Brady Lighting Design
Graphics	H Plus Incorporated
Acoustics/AV/Telecom	Cerami & Associates
Geotechnical/Civil	Langan Engineering and Environmental Services
Sustainable Design	Viridian Energy & Environmental
Security	Aggleton + Associates
Food Service	Hopkins Foodservice Specialists
Estimating	Wolf and Company
Elevator	Iros Elevator

CONSTRUCTION MANAGER
STV

BOOK CREDITS

Designers	Aislinn Weidele, Susan T. Rodriguez
Editor	Susan Strauss
Contributors	Brian Masuda, Reid Caudill, Marcela Villaroel-Trindade, Thomas Newman, Patricia Salas, Shuoan Zhou, Hiroko Nakatani

BUILDING PHOTOGRAPHY

Jeff Goldberg/ESTO: endpapers, 34, 37, 40-42, 48-50, 56, 58, 60, 66, 70-72, 76, 77, 78-79. 91
Aislinn Weidele/Ennead Architects: 45-46, 54, 57, 62, 65, 69, 74, 76, 80

OTHER IMAGES

Social Explorer: 11
Ennead Architects: 6, 8, 14, 16, 22, 25, 39, 52-53, 61, 65
Susan T. Rodriguez: 38

TEXTS

"Moving Your Institution Into the 21st Century" (excerpt), Joseph N. Hankin. Delivered to the College Board Conference, Valhalla, New York, November 13, 1990